Happy Birthday!

Birthday Party Games

by Sarah L. Schuette

Consulting editor: Gail Saunders-Smith, PhD

CAPSTONE PRESS
a capstone imprint

Pebble Plus is published by Capstone Press,
151 Good Counsel Drive, P.O. Box 669, Mankato, Minnesota 56002.
www.capstonepress.com

092009
005618CGS10

 Books published by Capstone Press are manufactured with paper
containing at least 10 percent post-consumer waste.

Library of Congress Cataloging-in-Publication Data
Schuette, Sarah L., 1976–
    Birthday party games / by Sarah L. Schuette.
    p. cm. — (Pebble plus. Happy birthday!)
    Includes bibliographical references and index.
    Summary: "Simple text and colorful photographs describe birthday party games" — Provided by publisher.
    ISBN 978-1-4296-4000-8 (library binding)
    1. Birthday parties — Juvenile literature. 2. Group games — Juvenile literature. I. Title.
GV1472.7.B5S385 2010
790.1'5 — dc22   2009026271

Editorial credits
Erika L. Shores, editor; Ashlee Suker, designer; Wanda Winch, media researcher; Eric Manske, production specialist;
    Sarah Schuette, photo stylist; Marcy Morin, scheduler

Photo credits
Capstone Studio/Karon Dubke, all

The Capstone Press Photo Studio thanks Countryside Homes, in Mankato, Minn., for their help with photo
    shoots for this book.

The author dedicates this book to her mother, Jane S. Schuette, who planned really fun birthday party games.

Note to Parents and Teachers

The Happy Birthday! set supports national social studies standards related to culture.
This book describes and illustrates birthday party games. The images support early readers
in understanding the text. The repetition of words and phrases helps early readers learn new
words. This book also introduces early readers to subject-specific vocabulary words, which are
defined in the Glossary section. Early readers may need assistance to read some words and to
use the Table of Contents, Glossary, Read More, Internet Sites, and Index sections of the book.

Table of Contents

Party Time

Happy birthday!

Let's play some party games.

5

Inside Games

Rain or shine, indoor games
are fun to play.
Eric fills his bingo card first.
Bingo!

The music stops
in musical chairs.
Ty can't find a chair.
He's out!

Everyone looks for prizes

in a treasure hunt.

Jane finds a pretty pencil.

Adam spins around
wearing a blindfold.
He can't peek, but he wins!
He pins the tail
on the donkey.

13

Outside Games

Let's play some games outside.

Friends run carefully in

an egg-and-spoon race.

Jake swings a bat

at the piñata.

It cracks open.

Everyone grabs candy.

Everyone hops up and down
as they jump in a sack race.
Will Carlos cross
the finish line first?

Your Birthday

Birthday games keep you moving and laughing. What games do you play on your birthday?

Glossary

blindfold — a strip of fabric that is put over someone's eyes so they cannot see

piñata — a decorated container that is filled with candy and small gifts

prize — a reward for winning a game

race — a test of how fast a person can run or move

sack — a bag used to hold something

treasure — items of value that have been hidden for a birthday game; treasure can be toys, money, and other gifts.

Read More

Easterling, Lisa. *Games*. Our Global Community. Chicago: Heinemann, 2007.

Elya, Susan Middleton. *F Is for Fiesta*. New York: G.P. Putnam's Sons, 2006.

Powell, Jillian. *A Birthday*. Why Is This Day Special? North Mankato, Minn.: Smart Apple Media, 2007.

Internet Sites

FactHound offers a safe, fun way to find Internet sites related to this book. All of the sites on FactHound have been researched by our staff.

Here's all you do:

Visit *www.facthound.com*

FactHound will fetch the best sites for you!

Index

Word Count: 129
Grade: 1
Early-Intervention Level: 16